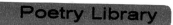

SUNSTREAMS

AND

SHADOWS

Cicely Rodway

Africa World Press, Inc.

P.O. Box 1892   P.O. Box 48

Trenton, NJ 08607   Asmara, ERITREA

Africa World Press, Inc.

P.O. Box 1892
Trenton, NJ 08607

P.O. Box 48
Asmara, ERITREA

Book design: Jonathan Gullery

This book is set in Bernhard Modern and Times New Roman

Library of Congress Cataloging-in-Publication Data

Rodway, Cicely.
    Sunstreams and shadows / Cicely Rodeway.
      p. cm.
    ISBN 0-86543-947-8 -- ISBN 0-86543-948-6 (pbk.)
      1. Women immigrants--Poetry. 2. Emigration and immigration--Poetry. I. Title.

PS3618.O36 S86 2001
811'.6--dc21   2001033363

DEDICATION

This collection is dedicated to the memory of my mother Mavis Alfreda Rodway, my father James Alwyn Rodway, (Sonny) my brother Leslie Brian Rodway and my aunts who mothered me Carmen Olive Bartrum and Lorna Rodway.

My friend Barbara Christian, who left us too early.

ACKNOWLEDGEMENTS

I would like to thank the following people who made this work possible:

My family : My sons, Mark and Frank Bobb who have seen me through the shadows and rejoiced with me in the sun times; my daughters, Leslie, Natalie and Vilna. Also Adrian, Rosalie, Hazel, Phyllis and Michael, Trevor and Debbie, Dianne. Cecilia Francis who said the magic words. Lorna Goodison who provided initial encouragement. The women of Fellowship Moravian Church, Brooklyn New York whose enthusiasm and support spurred me on. My friends who listened: Phyllis, Jessica, June, Bernice, Clairmonte, Eileen, Toby, Doreen, Annie Lee, Lorna, Sybil, Carol, Olivia, Helen, Marcia, Sonia, Maureen, Yemi, Paula, Denise, Joyce Andaiye. Professors Jeffry Allen, Tony O'Brien, Joan Nestle and Lindsay Patterson , Ali Jamile Ahmed; and my sisters in spirit Jeane Skeete and Bernadette Persaud whose support made *Sunstreams and Shadows* become a reality.

CONTENTS

DEDICATIONS 1

PRELUDE

Death of a Mother

Even before she died
she was already
removed from life
shut in
locked away in hospital
enveloped in politeness
as death
truth smothered hovered.

Numbed by her slow dying
love filled shielders
masked grieving
could not help her children
cushion their hearts for her leaving.

Who will tell her children?
Who will hold her children?
Who will hold her children close?
Find words to ease
their emptiness
their sorrow?

Deafened by flickering
heartbeats
no one could hear
her wilting bud children
who spoke
in many languages
in myriad ways.

Part 1

Motherchild

With death triumphant
Caregivers
now sorrow deafened
seemed not to hear
the leftbehind
motherchild
who spoke
in many languages
in myriad ways
who
lived in nightmare
waiting
waiting
for the
the nightmare
dreamlife's end.
Waited frozen
ice sculpted
poised
in pseudo-mother role
unaware of spewing
her own death seeds
in her mirroring
her mimicking
the selfless mother.

PART 2

On Hold

Nightmare dreamridden
the childmother slows
puts breathing
puts living on hold
in escrow.

Living in dream
breathstilled
she awaits her mother's return.
Heart mimic monitors kick in
pulse races frenetically
ensures existence
a paralleling
to counter breathstilling.

Masquerade selves
Manifest
Flourish
grotesque.

PART 3

Heartfrozen

Early mornings
gentle memory glimpses
of the absented mother
soon fade
as sunlight
bleeds into each day.

Dreaded daylight brings
wracking memory glimpses
of, the teutonic mother
gently smiling,
as in life
barely smiling
her gentlehearted smile.

Intermittently
motherchild glimpses
the smiling shadowrapped mother
Reclining in swaying branches
spread-eagled on ceilings
floating in eaved roofs.
Sitting in rear church pews
shadowsheathed
half veiled in the black diaphanous net
flowing from her favorite white felt hat.

Kneeling in front pew,
motherchild
senses her mother
turns slowly, very, very slowly
glimpses the mother
tries to catch her eye
entrap her in gaze
fails to stop her leaving
Abandonned, heartfrozen remains sedately kneeling
in front pew.

DEDICATIONS 2

You of the Fire

Alfred Jaggernauth Skeete hoped so much to see the "New Century" but died early, in February 1974

Eventually the dreaded truth
the crab had nibbled
had gnawed,
had taken so much
yet was not filled
and you,
you would never see the new one.

Beauty in your silence.
Your slow cat-like eyes smiled
"Courage I'm going to be all right."

Shorn of your mane
yet beautiful...
but perhaps
even then
some of you lost.
Savagely,
pain attacked your
burning bodymind beauty.

Swiftly you became
Parched
pain wracked
tortured into smiling.

You of the fire
you burnished bright
you could now only smile "courage."

Played Out

1987

Sprawled rather elegantly
in reachable chairs,
feigning a desire for
swift clean endings,
my father entertains.

1994

Thin wasted
almost inhuman in his frailty
my father lies motionless
atop immaculate pastel sheets
and neatly spread covers.

From time to time
his thin sinewy hands
claw the air
futile attempts to
exercise his now
arthritic fingers
which once
drew forth haunting blues rhythms
evoked Miles and Ellington
Shearing and Peterson
from the 1950 Sandemann upright.

Now silent,
it too
waits out its time
in the drawing room
where once flowed lifechatter
gossip, rerun soap operas,
lengthy political discussions
heated arguments.
All ended.
Played out
even before his life is over.

Few friends left.
Death, sickness
and fear of both
have whittled away at the numbers,
few eager to catch a mirroring of their own aging.

Brilliant mind
still alert
interred in the wraithlike frame.
Skin, almost translucent
meticulously cared for by a wife
with gnarled fingers
and strong memory riddled tongue.
Who along with gentle paid helpers
eases the playing out, the waiting.

Old Rod, Jays A, Slanty, Bowls,
shaper of mind,
politically fearless
unyielding in principle
remains verbally agnostic to the end.

Now consumed by life,
drained of the hope
of ever fishing again in
sunstreamed black waters
is played out.
Present shadows cover all.
Wants it over.
Lies atop the neatly spread sheets
waiting.

For Mavis

Of my Mother
Mavis the selfless
The gentle,
my Father's bluebell
lost early save
in memory
few words remembered.

But in my memoryimages
of lovedeeds
in her daily acts of caring
so many.

FRAGILITY

Fragility

Life's fragility
Came unexpectedly.
Not from endless
discourses
reading or reflection.

Rather,
in my own space
in the places nearest me
the possibility that one
could be empty.

Fear Creeps In

Fear creeps in on kitten paws
moves bellywise
upwards
gently.

Ascends
no longer gentle
mounting...mounting...mounting.

Callused tentacled paws
scrabbling,
scrambling upwards.
Morphosed
octupus-crabtiger
now paws
claws
heart wards
triumphant.

Terror

Corefrightened of being
she awaited her kismet
her mistress
her second-self.
Waited
unarmed
disarmed
knowledgeless of
ways to slay
the terror
the fear.

Fear swirled about her
clinging misty
creeping up
crept up
felt but unseen
seeped through
rooted
rooted deep.

Fearterror
needing to be fed.
cultivated spaces to feed.
fed
grew
fed
created.
Spawned
the seeds
the spreading branches of terror, Despair
Muted self-destruction.

Fear branched in her chest
owner of her breathing
showed itself
in nightmare
in waking
in changing forms
controlled
in diverse ways.

Til, overgrown...
Overridden...
she no longer knew
where she began.........
or ended.

Sunlessness

Sunlessness
soundlessness
each dulled day
painfilled.

Niggling
nebulous
pervasive death whimpers
shroud breath.
Too weak for
clear decisions
clean
finality action.

Grim days
barren nights
riddled with drear.
Slowed numbed responses
feigned desires.

Morning glimpse
of sunlight soon darkens
shadows all.

AFTER LOVE

After Love

Emptied but
for the children.
Desire slaked.
Terrified of heartsharing
of tearing and being torn.
Fearful of again
replacing lovedreams
with
seething hollowness.

Loose Ends

This will go on
till I
really try
to untie
this raveling cord
which now binds us.

I loveneed you
but not as then.
Now only
loosened heartstrings
muted
responses.

Night Shades

Taught early to
let not night shades
lie with you
and darken your mornings
you pursued the right ones
the acceptable light ones.
Settled only for
the pale, light
right ones.

Dead Loves

Dreams flood his nights
with the debris of his past
loves lost...forfeited...aborted...killed.
Dreams of his dead
his deadloves returning
to council
to criticize
and
as in life
seldom to praise.

Conquest

Fear not.
nothing to fear
unless the lover
feeds on conquest
breeds fear
kills trust
enthrones
the time of trust.

Beached

No melodies ring
no melodies ring
no drums beat.
Rhythm is stilled.
People shells strewn
across the sand
musicless

Shadows

Glad was I
when you said unto me
Come fly with me.
Together, cloud gliding
moon soaring.
Fear of flying
surging through
overwhelming.
Fore-shadows looming.
"Laugh today, cry tomorrow."
Shadowing the present
the desperate need to know
no tomorrow
will end
without you.

Lament

Whispers
Just whispers
just whispers of love.
Whispers and whimpers
You whimper for love.
Whispering, whimpering
endlessly whispering
prayerfully whispering
Whimpers for love.

Marriage Bonds

The bondage of marriage
scrolled the wife
listing
cataloging
the well rehearsed
wifely tribulations
including the support
the intermittent support.

The bondage of marriage
hissed the husband
rote chanting his list
his inventory.
The house, the car
The dogs,
the second car
the children
the garden
the support
the uneven support.

Bonded tension.
Wife and husband.
Lover and loveress
Wolf and wolverine.
Exquisite fettered bonding
daily flesh stripping
slicing
bitty slivers
imperceptibly demolishing
the original.

LOVE BRIGHT

For a New Love

Love has come
unexpectedly
and truth filled.
Has torn open
Closed spaces
No longer
Needed hiding places
No longer needed
Now that love has come
Has come, has come
unrushed.
Creating
building
gentle joy wisps
wisps of joy
worth waking for.

Love Bright

Love is in my blood
and I am new.
High
pure
anguished
pain strums through.
gentler than throbbing.

Sweet
sweet death pain sweetness
quickens
quickens
slowly urging
slower yet quickened breath.
Piercing sweetness surges
with memories of touches
of touching
of nearness
of closeness
of death defying warmth.
Of rapture in every
emptied heart space
now filled
with love bright times
with you.

The Eagle Wind

The eagle wind
at first gently soaring
ruffling your coolth
riffling your depth
'Til you were caught
in the tumult
of the now raging wings.
Circling, soaring.
No clamping patterns
No crushing
No encaging.
Free flowing
Wings enfolding
No crushing.

No Words

Clutching for comfort
at night
when dream becomes nightmare
and nightmare dream
no words offered
no words needed.

Acheburning for comfort
Fumbling for closeness
no words
bodies showed how
no words.

TO LIFT THE VEIL

Gendered

Constructed to live
gendered existences
form existences
blank space lives

Women struggle to
fill in the blanks
eliminate duty tasks
preordained life tasks
assigned roles.

Gentle - Man

Your gentleness labeled tainted
tinged with female
tarnished with woman
unacceptable
unmale.

Your labelers' empty heartminds
swamped by whispers
understandings
spawned behind
cupped
truth hiding palms,
decry
denounce consummations
unsanctioned by narrow codes.

Spewing, corralled
herdlike sharing
of programmed
judgments.
Fearfullness
fueled by
edicts
learned
on families tight closed knees
on constricted narrow benches
of learning and worship.

Foremothers

Foremothers
always smiling
save when,
they screamed inside,
wrung through with the living
the overflowing
the required selfless
raising of children.
The daily dulling child raising
which left no place,
no space for their own raising
no nurturing of their talents.

No creations
save children.
Imagination funneled into cooking,
baking lightly sugared buns.
Sewing children's garments
knitting. . . . tatting
embroidering flowers
on outfits for
special occasions.

Visibly serene.
Seeming to desire nothing
but motherwife accolades
gifts on birthdays
church on Sundays.
Seeming to desire nothing more.

To Lift the Veil

Though veil-less
veiled.
Tradition shrouded
Gendered
Culture forged...stamped.
Still nameless to self
Faceless
Emerging
embattled
struggling
to lift
to mangle her veil.

WORLDS AWAY
FROM HOME

Immigrant Woman

Immigrant woman
balances precariously
on window ledge.
Heady summer breezes
lull her,
evoke another time
another life
staunch loss
calm her
move her back
beyond the flawed immediate,
the acceptance of scarred choices
numbing daily acceptance
of faceless margin living.

If the Truth be Known

*For a friend who migrated to New York to pave the way for
children and husband. For my friend who "lived in" to pave
the way. For my friend who I lost along the way.*

Changed...Changed...Changed
no certainties.
Who will face her
enfold her
who will embrace her
if the truth be known?

If the truth be known?
will all turn
hide their faces
reclaim their hearts
their love?
Shun me,
will they shun me?
Shun me. Shun me...
Shun me...
SHHHH......Shun me
if the truth be known?

If the truth be known
surely they will
blame my sway
my sashay
my choosing late on
Sunday's summer evenings to
meander slowly workwards
to gently dream my way
through lawned,

treelined
trellised streets
when
summer smells
flood me with memories
of my land
my home of never ending summer
my homeland where my children
exist
awaiting my return.

Headbent
she ponders the telling.
Fearful of truthspilling
Dreading
the whispers
the shame
the shunning
by those who once
enfolded her.
The homeland husband
who will blame her sway
her provocative sashay,
if the truth be known.

Color Dialog

You're colored.

Colored what?

Mixed.

Mixed with what? Wood spoon or metal?

This is no joke.

Isn't it?

You are a mulatto.

Mulatto!!! Mulatto! Genesis - mule
engineered
unnatural
reproduction nil
rolebred to serve
disempowered, neuter.

Why this black thing?

Here in this US of A,
on the books, just one drop.

Your mother's white

My father's black

Choose:
tawny/brown/
tawnybrown
brightred/redbright
yellow/light
high yellow
colored light
mixed/almost white
mustee/fustee/dustee/
rusty/rustee.
Not black,
cause you're not pure black.

Never said pure.
Only white pure.
Only said black,
more than a color black.

Ebony Madonna

For Debbie Rodway

Gentleness
pervades this Ebony Madonna's
body and spirit.
Deep calm
her trademark.
Unshakeable faith in
a benevolent universe
despite a reality of
bypasses,
urban challenges
and motherhood of children
marked in skin
by slave
and slave master.

Seemingly emotionless
devoid of bitterness
she recounts
in surreal tones
how,
in public places
her motherhood is questioned
and she is cautioned
to care well
her paid charges,
"the little dolls."
"the little dolls so light."

Worlds Away from Home

Looking out at snow-capped trees
in the heart of Queens, Jamaica,
worlds away from home
yet home
the heartmind trembles,
rails at the ceilings
lowered on those
for whom the Lady's torch
does not shine bright.

In the heart of Jamaica
worlds away from home
glimpses of possibilities
sporting chances
level fields
equal odds
dreams of undeferred dreams
fuel the need to challenge
the rigid ceilings
erected for the hounded
lowered on the shadowed
the old new prey
crouched
cramped
manacled
confined by carefully erected
low ceilings
in this new world
where the Lady's lamp shines
shines brightly
only on the chosen.

Inner City Death

Slow death
birthed by dream-killed lives
birthed in death.
Slow death
incremental.

Minds and souls
shrink.
Heart
mind
soul
shrunken.
Dream emptied lives
lived out
unlived.

Ambushed by Memories

The Past Surfaces

The past
surfaces in
faces of teachers
past teachers
old in years
and in living.

Now
masks lifted
tongues softened
people emerge.

Emotion
once
stifled
in rigid classrooms
finally surfaces.

Coming Home

Voice rhythms
voices in rhythm
in tune, with you
lull you home.

Little has changed.
Clean fresh air fills each room.
Soothing sea tinged breezes
encircle all.
The green kettle
no whistle,
boils slowly for tea.
Green tea - Red Rose or Liptons.
Or, if you prefer rum and or cherry juice.

Talk never ending
fills the days
the nights
the gentle breezy mornings.
Sun low in the clear blue sky
no haze here.

Rum and tea and talk and
tea and rum and talk
and peace and calm.
Your neighbor putters in his garden
stops to chat, has time, makes time
finds time, can stop.

You're home where
people find time to chat.
You're home
You know you're home
When people stop to chat
to drink with you
a cup of tea
a shot of rum,
a glass of cherry juice.

Ambushed by Memories

Reflections on the first reading of "Web of Secrets"
by Denise Harris

Perched, edgy,
a little bird herself
not brightly plumed.
Swathed in shades of brown
rich brown
and black and red
the red she chose
to brighten things up a bit.

Brightly she burned, while
drawing us to her memories
entrapping us in her web.

She read of an unnamed country
whose name we knew.
Of light people
colorless people
people without color
people heavy with color.

Of the wistful child
seeking to know
listening to know
to learn
the hidden truths
the secrets locked so far away
since times of ambush
out of Africa.
Secrets of a family
secrets of a people
ambushed by life.

In right shadowed corner
turned wallwards
a colorless woman listened
turned away,
remained apart
from those she knew not.
Yet, she did enter with the writer
the writer wreathed in earth tones
reading of the lives
of the living
in the unnamed land.
Reading of the mother
who once burned bright
flickered
soon died.

The colorless woman
unnamed
foreign
circled
by "the others"
remained apart.

Scribbling, scribbling.
mothermothermothermother
mothermothermothermother
silently weeping
silently scribbling,
weepingsilentlysilentlyweeping
silent tears
uneasily accepted
the comfort tissues
of silent empathy.
pressed on her.

This setapart
separate woman
disconnected by history
and choosing
exited at the end.
Vanished unnamed.

Ambushed by memories
fettered by history
Marked in memory
colored in
in memory
remembered only by her weeping

BRING IN THE SUN

How Soon

For my sons, Mark and Frank Bobb

How soon have come
The hard virile bodies
muscled arms
sculpted bodies
wisps of beards
and mustaches.
evolving chameleonlike
casting off childskins.
boyhood mannerisms.

New challenges
and uncertainties
fearless experimentation
foster
adult introspection
reflectiveness
bringing
new understandings
of love's
responsibilities
relationship to family.

Bring in the Sun

We must bring in the sun
dismantle the nets
give praise,
not negatives
to keep them afloat
in this hostile
vacuous society.

Praise
not censure
guided by fear of sparing the rod
of spoiling the child
will catapult our children upstream.

We must
embrace
their daily triumphs
recognize
their struggles
their battles with
circumscribed jaded curricula
ingrained attitudes
prejudices
low expectations
which exclude excellence.

Too often our children
are netted into schools
delivered to classrooms
to be molded and marred.
Amoeboid like they glide
aimlessly drift
over...under...around...
never fully in.

Then cast out
they float.
Buoyed by abyss images
truly adrift
they can only
clutch at each other
to make hate
make death
make love
make bored
angerfilled
cynical lives
unless we bring in the sun.

Sun Children

For Amina and Jared

Sun children
bright hued sunfilled flowers
shed sunsplashed beauty.
Bring sunlight
amber stars and moonsuns
Sun children fill
Life's cup to overflowing
With their brilliance
life rhythms
with the brightness
with joy.